Jazz Classics
50 Favorites from the Bebop Era and Beyond

Photography by Peter Amft

ISBN 0-634-04798-1

HAL•LEONARD®
CORPORATION
7777 W. BLUEMOUND RD. P.O. BOX 13819 MILWAUKEE, WI 53213

Visit Hal Leonard Online at
www.halleonard.com

Jazz Classics

CONTENTS

AIREGIN

By SONNY ROLLINS

Fast Swing

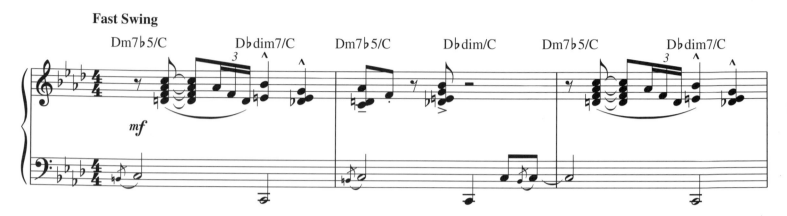

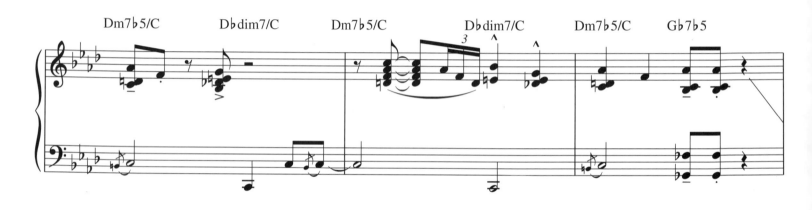

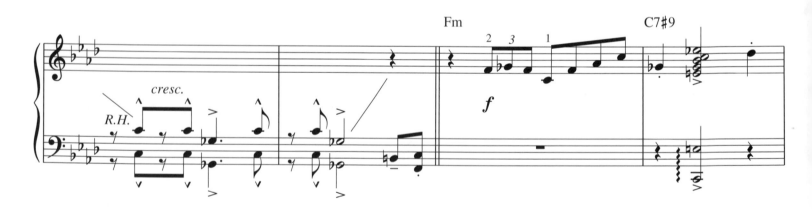

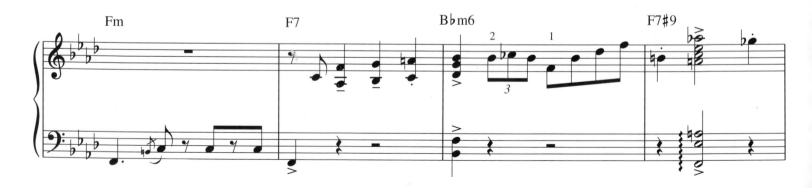

AU PRIVAVE

By CHARLIE PARKER

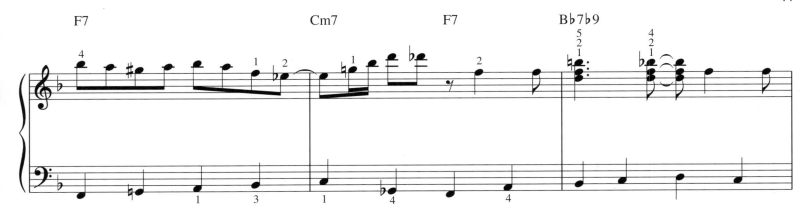

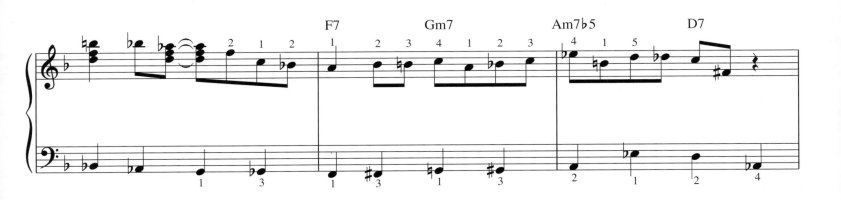

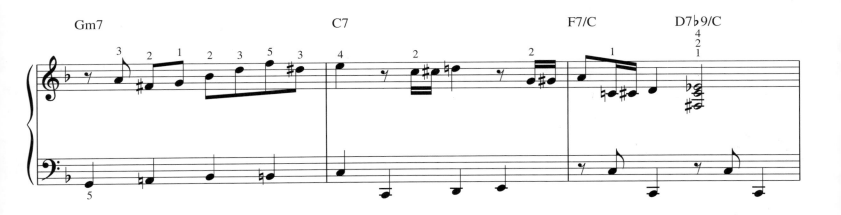

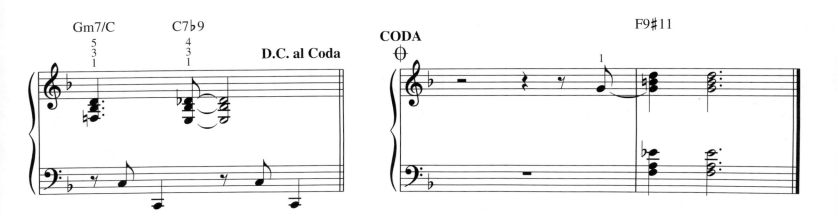

ALL BLUES

By MILES DAVIS

BAGS' GROOVE

By MILT JACKSON

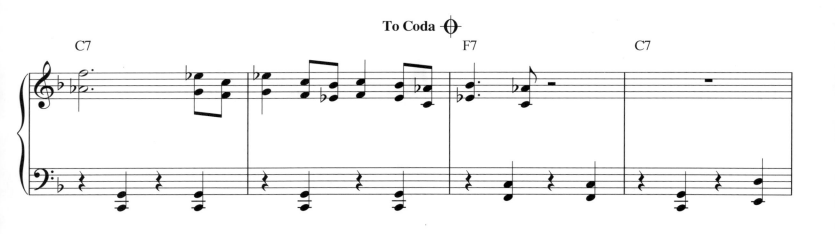

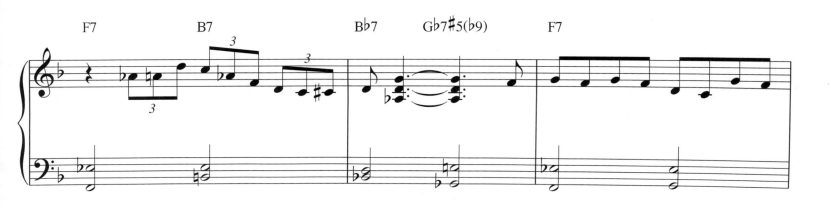

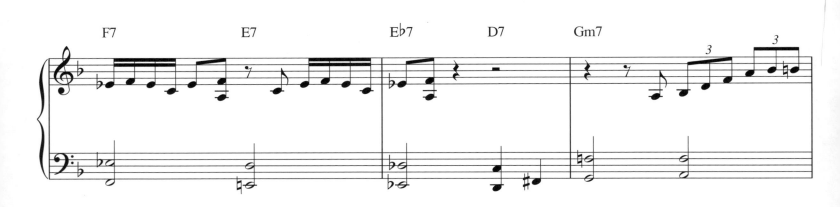

BIRK'S WORKS

By DIZZY GILLESPIE

BLUE TRAIN
(Blue Trane)

By JOHN COLTRANE

BLUE BOSSA

By KENNY DORHAM

Moderate Latin

To Coda ⊕

BLUE IN GREEN

By MILES DAVIS

A CHILD IS BORN

By THAD JONES
and ALEX WILDER

Slow Waltz

To Coda

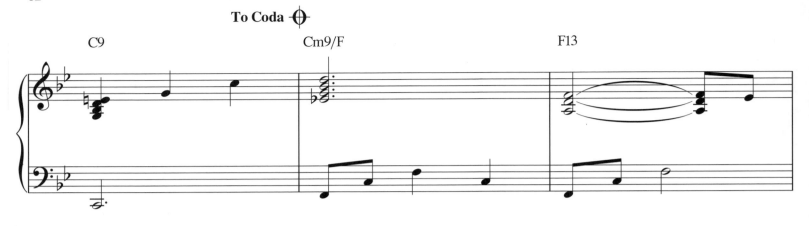

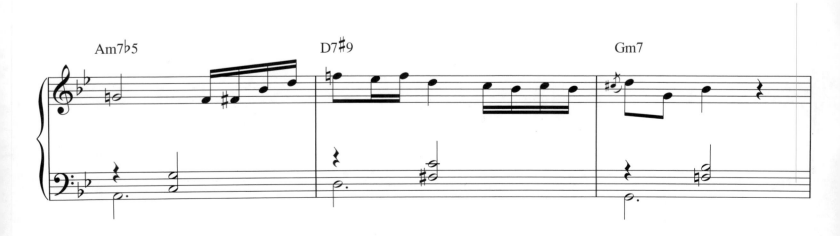

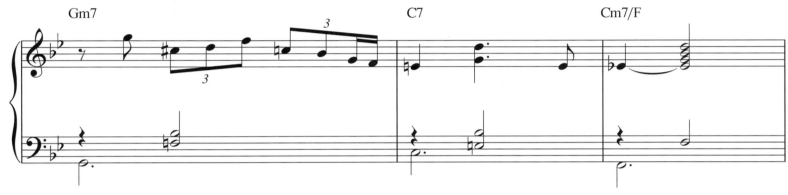

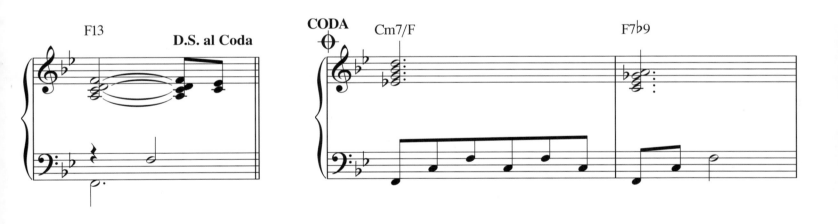

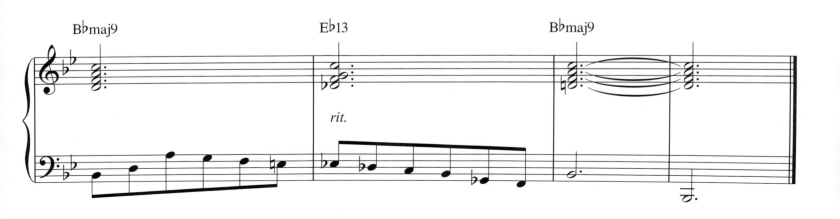

CON ALMA

By JOHN "DIZZY" GILLESPIE

DAT DERE

By BOBBY TIMMONS

Medium Swing

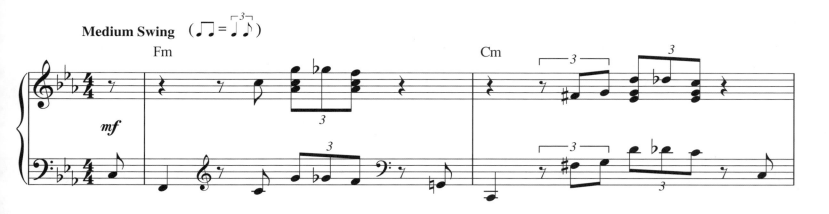

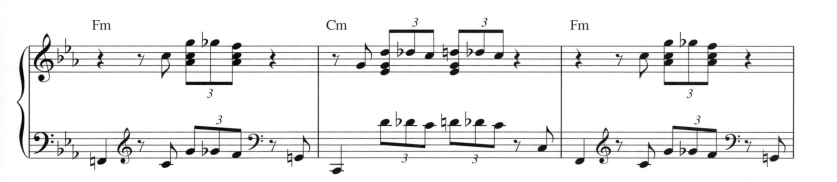

CONFIRMATION

By CHARLIE PARKER

DOXY

By SONNY ROLLINS

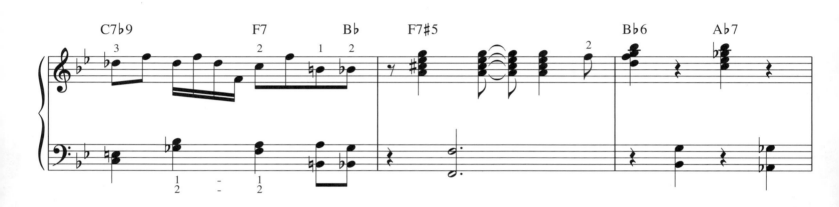

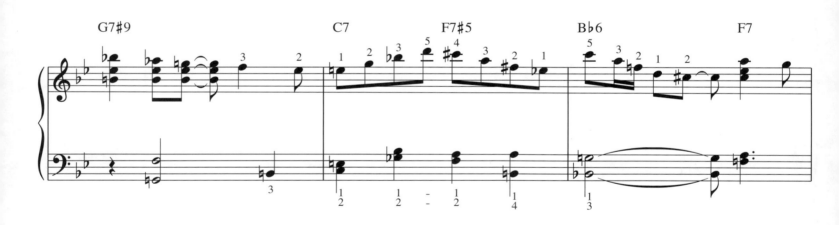

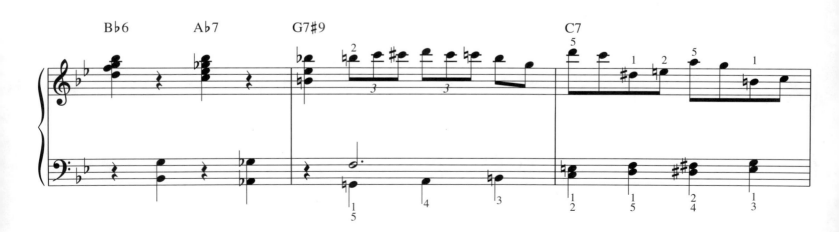

DREAMY

Music by ERROLL GARNER
Lyric by SYDNEY SHAW

Ask me why I have this smile up-on my face,_ Ask me
why I see a rain-bow out in space,_ Well, I
must con - fess,_____ you don't need a ge-nius to guess

EPISTROPHY

By THELONIOUS MONK
and KENNY CLARK

FOOTPRINTS

By WAYNE SHORTER

Moderate Swing

FOUR

By MILES DAVIS

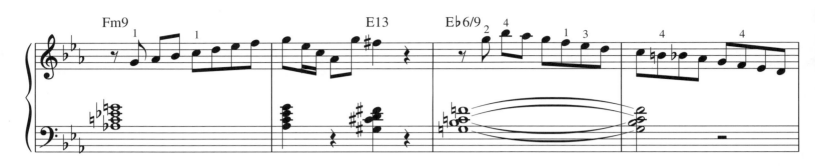

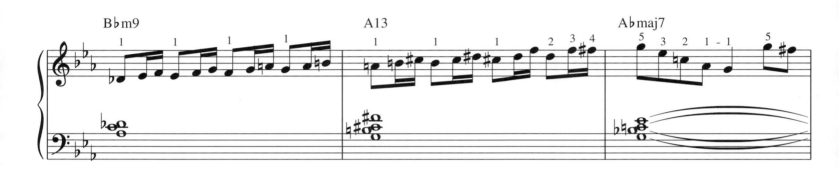

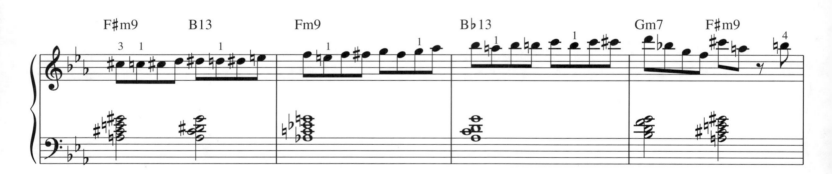

D.S. al Fine

FREDDIE FREELOADER

By MILES DAVIS

GIANT STEPS

By JOHN COLTRANE

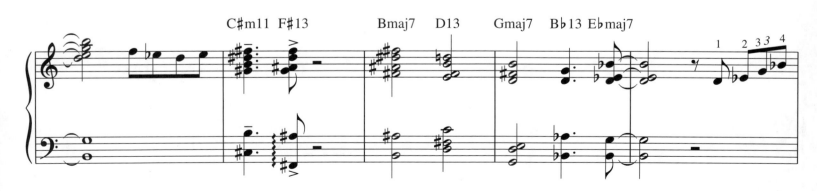

IN WALKED BUD

By THELONIOUS MONK

THE GIFT!
(Recado Bossa Nova)

Music by DJALMA FERREIRA
Original Lyric by LUIZ ANTONIO
English Lyric by PAUL FRANCIS WEBSTER

ISRAEL

By JOHN CARISI

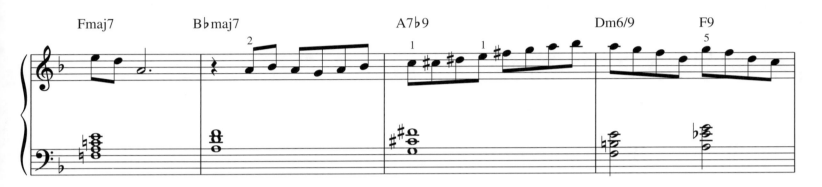

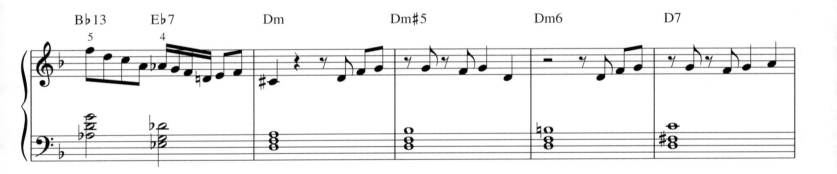

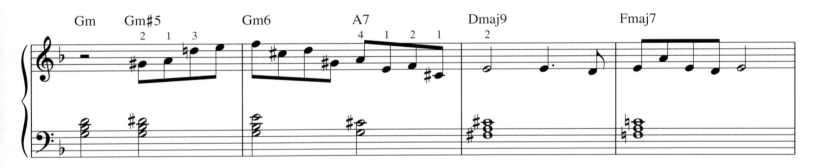

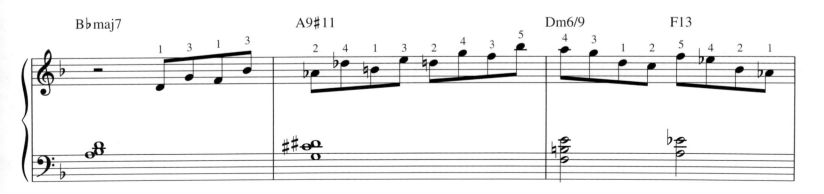

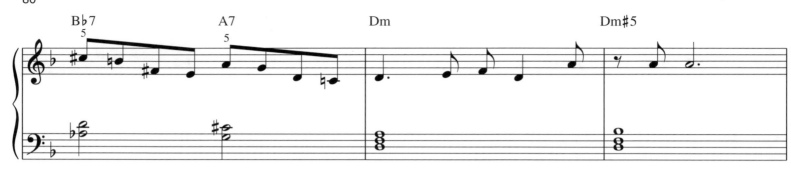

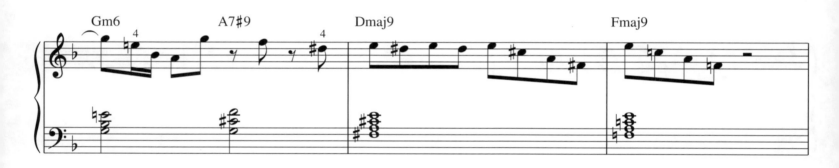

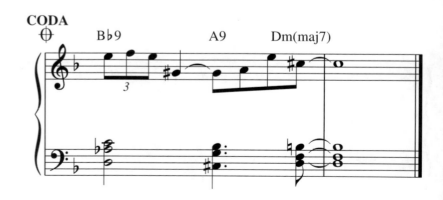

THE JIVE SAMBA

By NAT ADDERLEY

KILLER JOE

By BENNY GOLSON

MANTECA

By DIZZY GILLESPIE, WALTER GIL FULLER
and LUCIANO POZO GONZALES

Moderate Latin

8vb

LADY BIRD

By TADD DAMERON

MERCY, MERCY, MERCY

Composed by JOSEF ZAWINUL

Slow Funky Rock

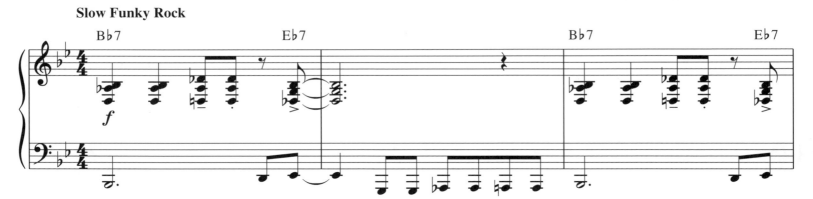

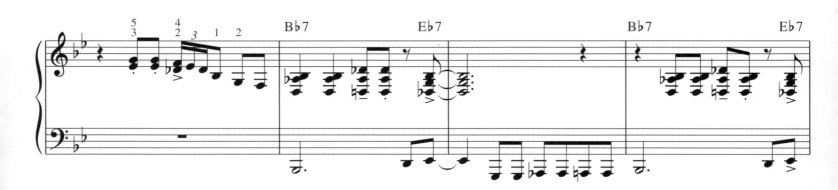

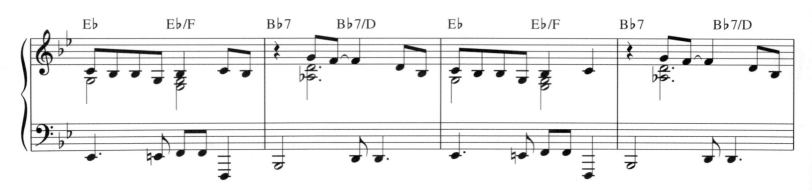

RED CLAY

By FREDDIE HUBBARD

Moderate Rock

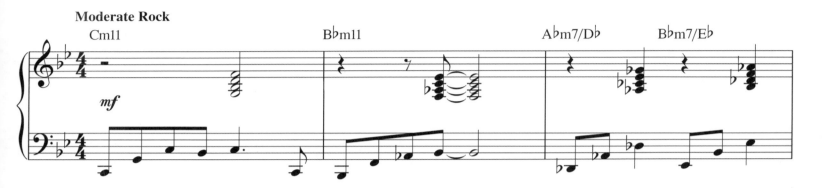

MOANIN'

By BOBBY TIMMONS

NAIMA
(Niema)

By JOHN COLTRANE

To Coda ⊕

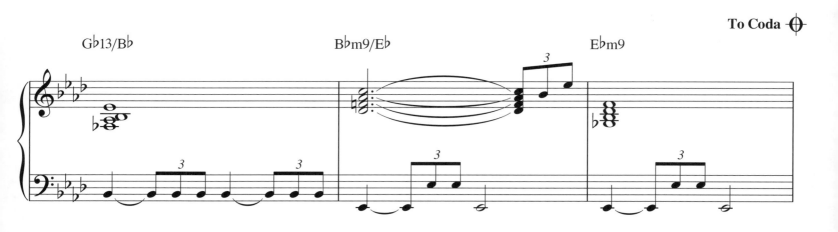

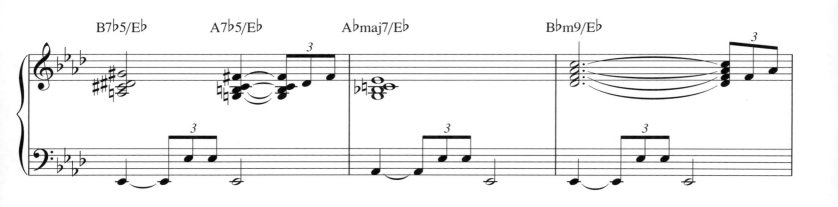

NARDIS

By MILES DAVIS

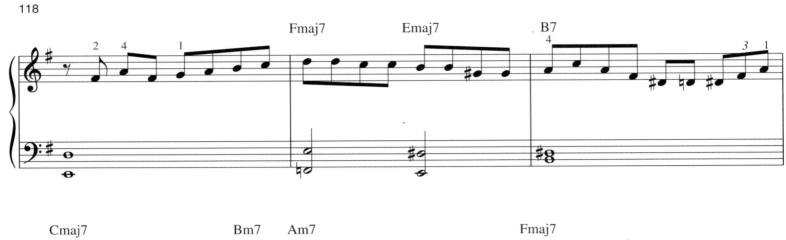

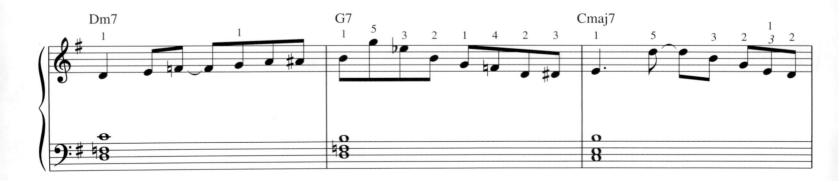

OLEO

By SONNY ROLLINS

ORNITHOLOGY

By CHARLIE PARKER
and BENNIE HARRIS

Moderate Jazz tempo

PHASE DANCE

By PAT METHENY
and LYLE MAYS

Moderately fast

N.C.

mf

With pedal

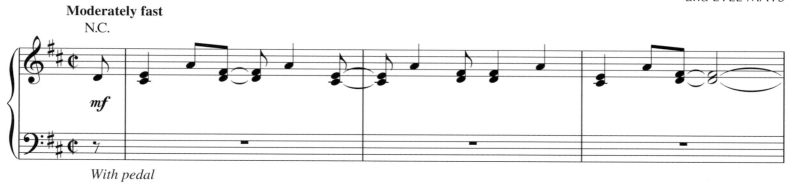

Bm9

L.H. one octave lower throughout

B♭maj7#11

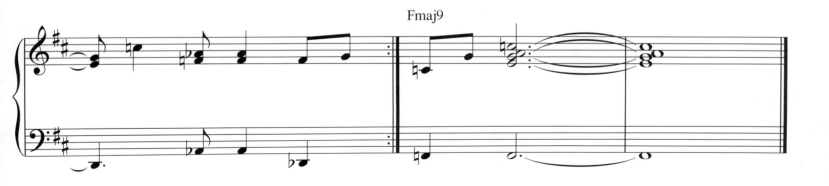

ROAD SONG

By JOHN L. (WES) MONTGOMERY

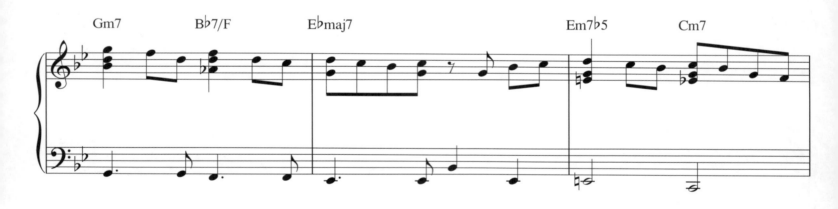

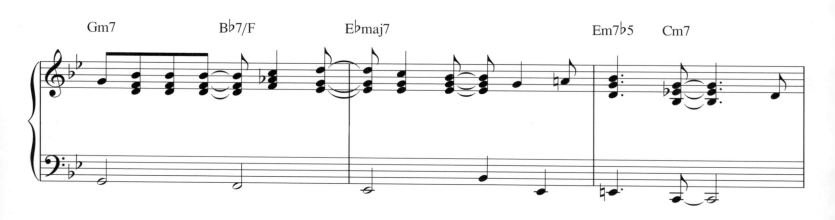

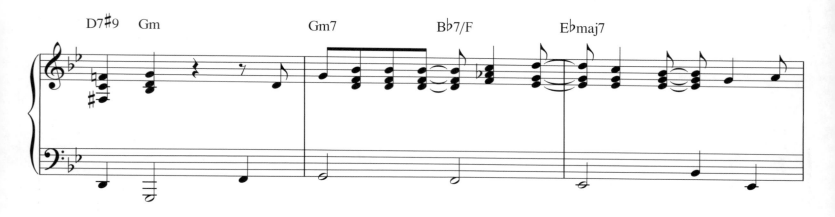

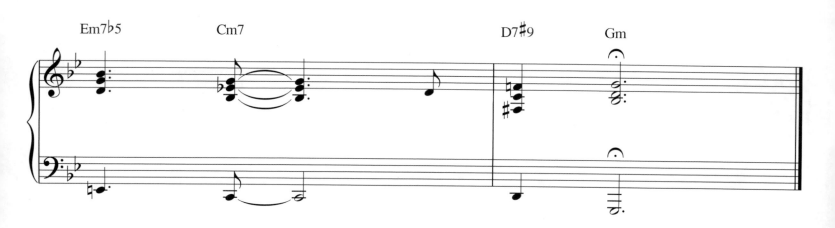

SEVEN STEPS TO HEAVEN

By MILES DAVIS
and VICTOR FELDMAN

'ROUND MIDNIGHT

Words by BERNIE HANIGHEN
Music by THELONIOUS MONK
and COOTIE WILLIAMS

Moderately slow, in 2

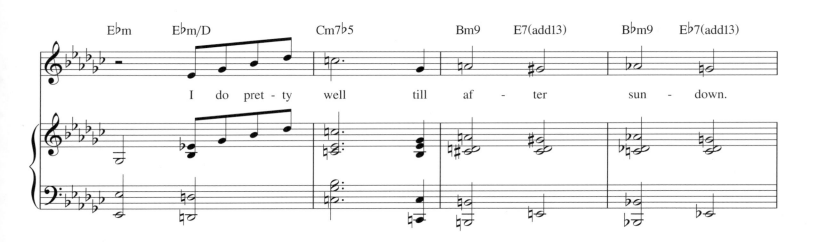

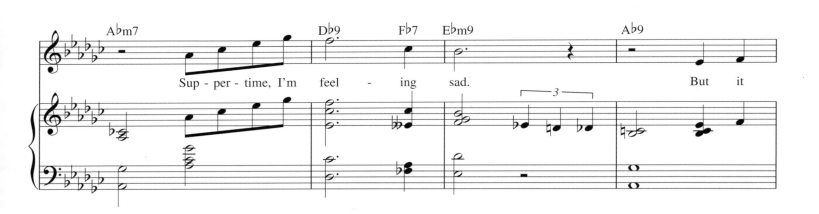

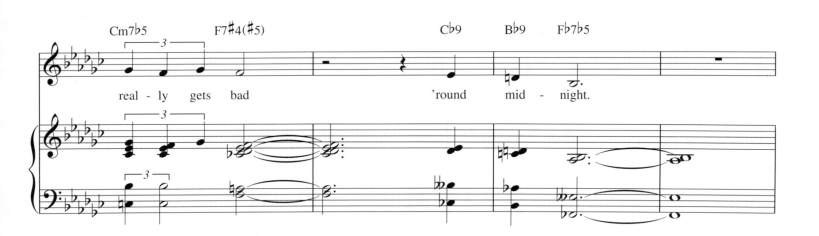

144

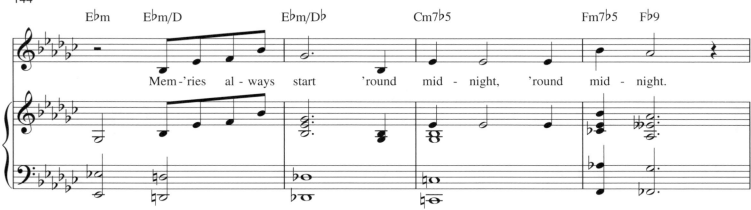

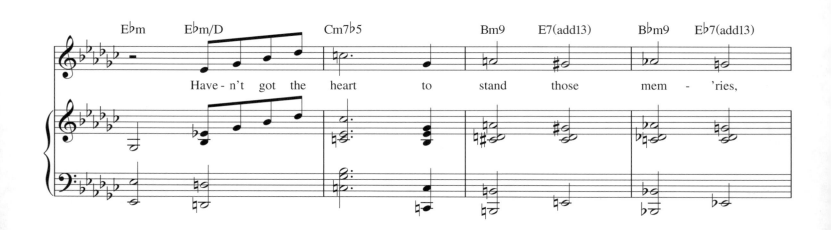

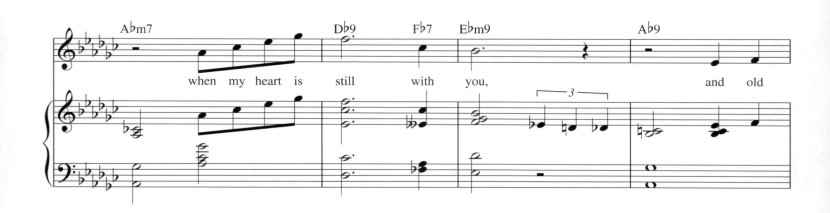

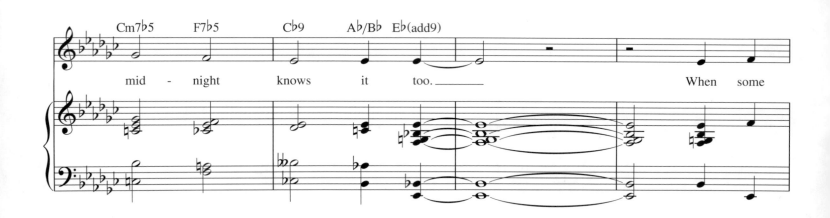

146

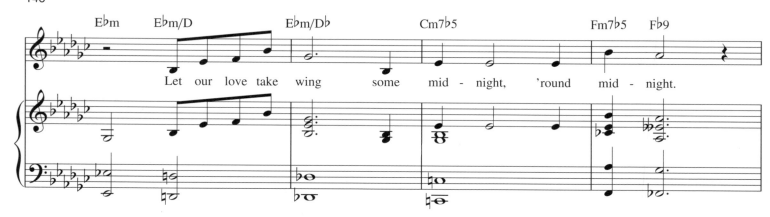

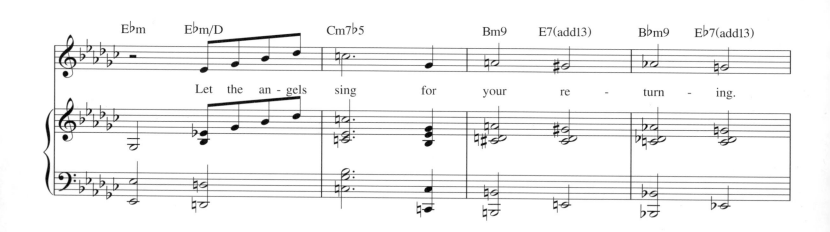

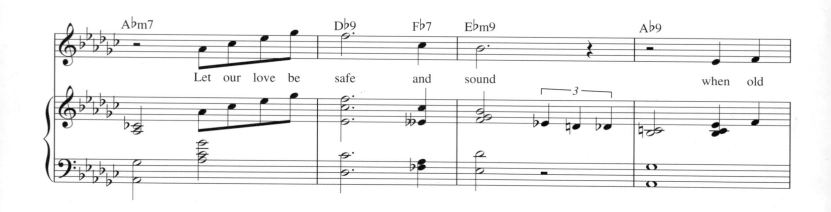

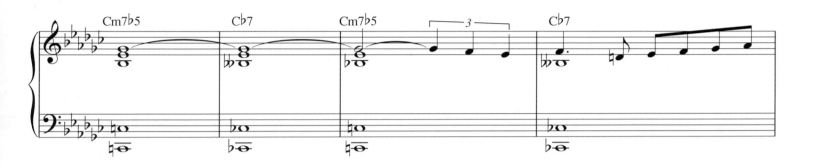

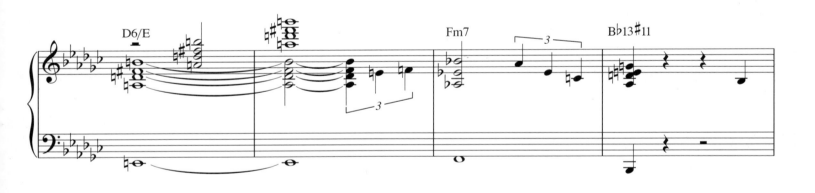

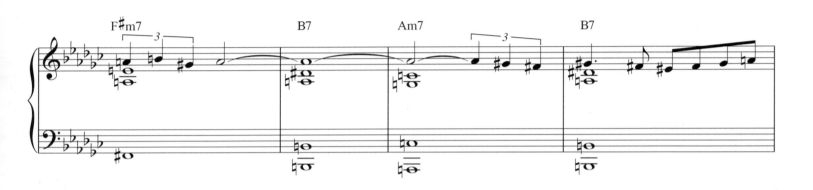

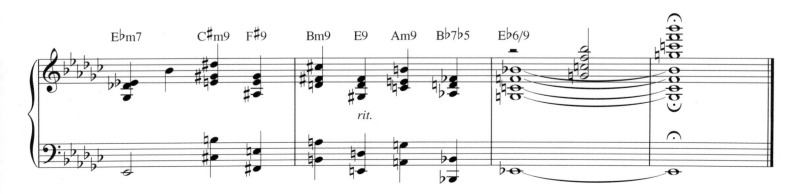

RUBY, MY DEAR

By THELONIOUS MONK

ST. THOMAS

By SONNY ROLLINS

Moderate Calypso

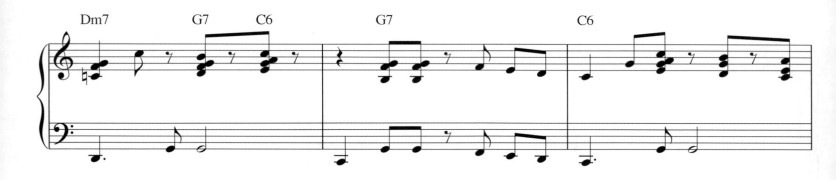

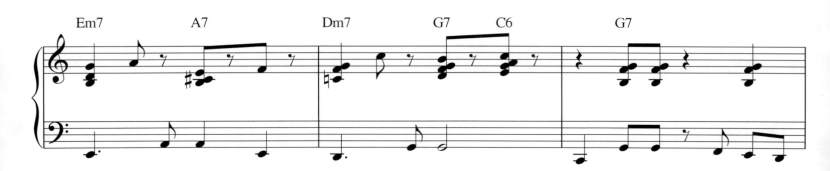

To Coda

SCRAPPLE FROM THE APPLE

By CHARLIE PARKER

SIDEWINDER

By LEE MORGAN

SO WHAT

By MILES DAVIS

SONG FOR MY FATHER

By HORACE SILVER

Moderate Bossa Nova

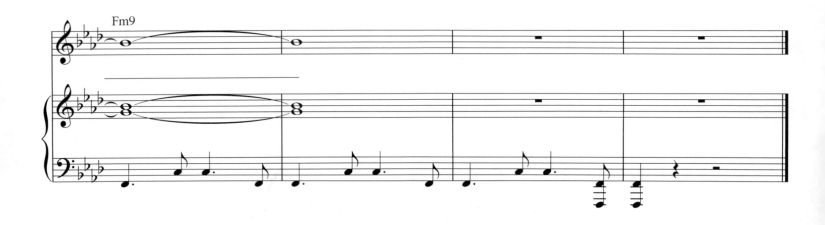

SPEAK NO EVIL

By WAYNE SHORTER

Moderately

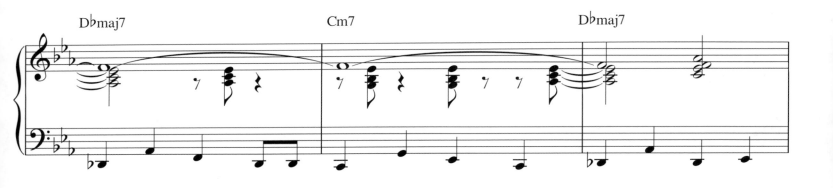

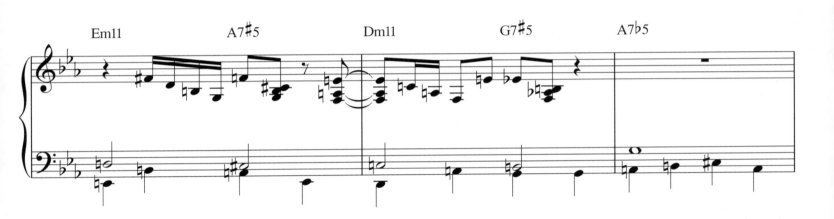

D.S. al Coda

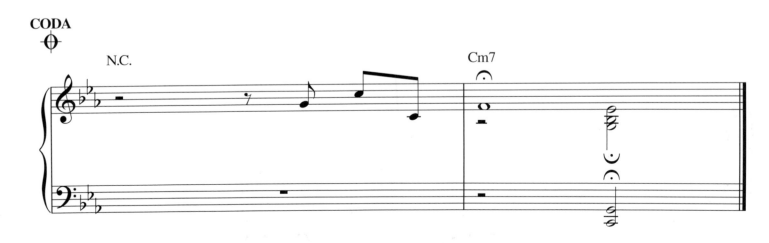

TAKE FIVE

By PAUL DESMOND

TUNE UP

By MILES DAVIS

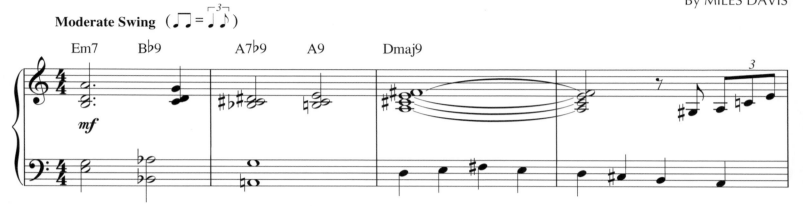

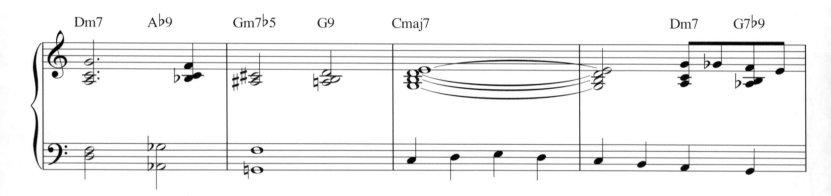

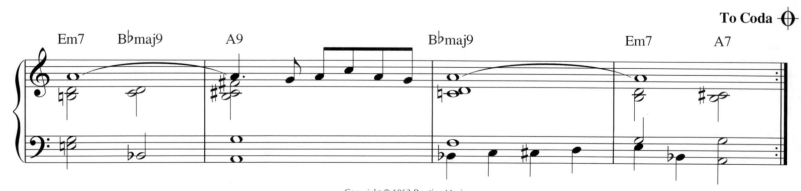

WALTZ FOR DEBBY

Lyric by GENE LEES
Music by BILL EVANS

WOODYN' YOU

By DIZZY GILLESPIE

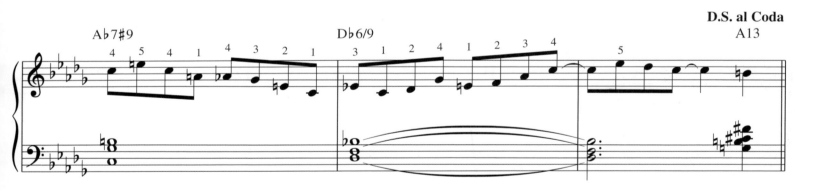

WELL YOU NEEDN'T
(It's Over Now)

English Lyric by MIKE FERRO
Music by THELONIOUS MONK

Medium Swing

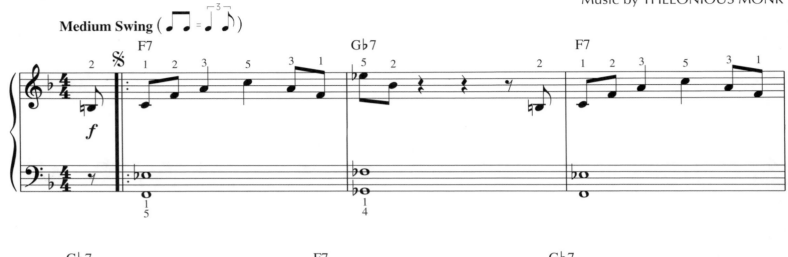

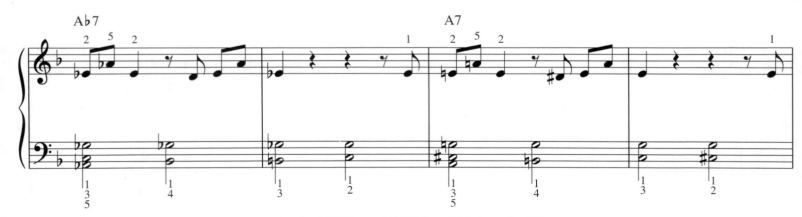

YARDBIRD SUITE

By CHARLIE PARKER

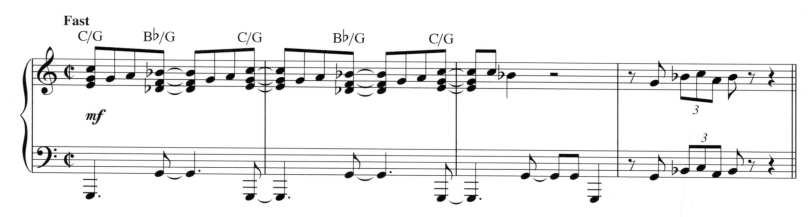

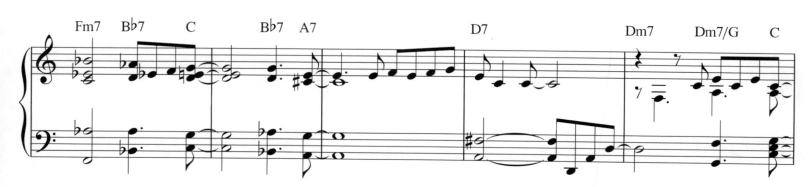

REAL JAZZ FAKE BOOKS FROM HAL LEONARD

These magnificent compilations hold over 240 standards of jazz repertoire in each book, containing easy-to-read authentic hand-written jazz engravings. The collections also feature the original harmony, and an alternate harmonization reflecting common practice by many jazz artists, so players can choose to use the traditional version, a hipper version, or a combination of the two! Spiral comb bound.

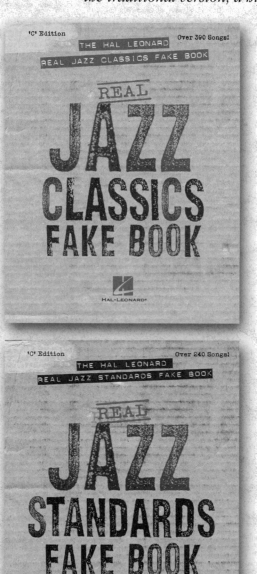

THE HAL LEONARD REAL JAZZ CLASSICS BOOK

Over 300 classic jazz hits, including: After the Rain • Airegin • All Blues • Along Came Betty • Ana Maria • Bags' Groove • Billie's Bounce (Bill's Bounce) • Birdland • Blues in Hoss Flat (Foster/Basie) • Boplicity (Be Bop Lives) • The Champ • Chelsea Bridge • A Child Is Born • Don't Be That Way • Emancipation Blues • Epistrophy • Footprints • Freddie Freeloader • Giant Steps • Half Nelson • I Waited for You • In Walked Bud • Israel • Johnny Come Lately • Jordu • Jump, Jive An' Wail • Lady Bird • Lemon Drop • Line for Lyons • Little Waltz • Lullaby of Birdland • Mambo #5 • Miles • Naima (Niema) • A Night in Tunisia • One for Daddy • Passion Flower • Peel Me a Grape • Quiet Now • Red Top • Robin's Nest • Rosewood • Ruby, My Dear • Seven Come Eleven • Sidewinder • So Far Away • So What • Song for Helen • Stolen Moments • Take Five • Tenor Madness • Time Remembered • Waltz for Debby • Well You Needn't (It's over Now) • Yardbird Suite • and more.

_____	00240162 C Edition	$39.95
_____	00240174 B♭ Edition	$39.95
_____	00240175 E♭ Edition	$39.95

THE HAL LEONARD REAL JAZZ STANDARDS FAKE BOOK

246 songs, including: Ain't Misbehavin' • Angel Eyes • Bein' Green • Blue Skies • Brazil • Cherokee (Indian Love Song) • Crazy He Calls Me • Darn That Dream • Desafinado (Off Key) • Early Autumn • Easy Living • Fever • For Every Man There's a Woman • Girl Talk • Good Morning Heartache • Here's That Rainy Day • How Little We Know • I Can't Give You Anything but Love • I Didn't Know What Time It Was • I Got It Bad and That Ain't Good • I Remember You • I'll Be Around • I'm Beginning to See the Light • I've Heard That Song Before • Imagination • It Could Happen to You • It's Easy to Remember • June in January • Lazy Afternoon • Midnight Sun • My Blue Heaven • My One and Only Love • Mood Indigo • Moonglow • One for My Baby (And One More for the Road) • Satin Doll • Sophisticated Lady • Star Dust • Tenderly • When Sunny Gets Blue • and more. Spiral comb bound.

_____	00240161 C Edition	$39.95
_____	00240173 B♭ Edition	$39.95
_____	00240172 E♭ Edition	$39.95

FOR MORE INFORMATION, SEE YOUR LOCAL MUSIC DEALER, OR WRITE TO:

HAL•LEONARD® CORPORATION

7777 W. BLUEMOUND RD. P.O. BOX 13819 MILWAUKEE, WI 53213

Visit Hal Leonard Online at
www.halleonard.com

Prices, contents and availability subject to change without notice.

KEYBOARD STYLE SERIES

These book/CD packs provide focused lessons that contain valuable how-to insight, essential playing tips, and beneficial information for all players. Comprehensive treatment is given to each subject, complete with a companion CD, which features many of the examples in the book performed either solo or with a full band.

BEBOP JAZZ PIANO
THE COMPLETE GUIDE
by John Valerio

In this book, author John Valerio provides essential, detailed information for bebop and jazz keyboardists on the following topics: chords and voicings, harmony and chord progressions, scales and tonality, common melodic figures and patterns, comping, characteristic tunes, the styles of Bud Powell and Thelonious Monk, and much more. The accompanying CD features many of the examples in the book performed either solo or with a full band. Also included are combo performances of five of the tunes featured at the end of the book.

00290535 Book/CD Pack..$16.95

ROCK KEYBOARDS
THE COMPLETE GUIDE
by Scott Miller

Rock Keyboard is chock full of authentic rock keyboard parts. Learn to comp or solo in any of your favorite rock styles. Listen to the CD to hear your parts fit in with the total groove of the band. Includes 99 tracks! Covers: classic rock, pop/rock, blues rock, Southern rock, hard rock, progressive rock, alternative rock, and heavy metal.

00310823 Book/CD Pack..$14.95

ROCK & ROLL PIANO
THE COMPLETE GUIDE
by Andy Vinter

With this pack, you'll learn the skills you need to take your place alongside Fats Domino, Jerry Lee Lewis, Little Richard, and other great rock 'n' roll piano players of the '50s and '60s! CD includes demos and backing tracks so you can play along with every example. Also includes six complete tunes at the end of the book! Covers: left-hand patterns; basic rock 'n' roll progressions; right-hand techniques; straight eighths vs. swing eighths; glisses, crushed notes, rolls, note clusters, and more; how to solo; influential players, styles and recordings; and much more!

00310912 Book/CD Pack..$14.95

STRIDE & SWING PIANO
THE COMPLETE GUIDE
by John Valerio

Learn the styles of the masters of stride and swing piano, such as Scott Joplin, Jimmy Yancey, Pete Johnson, Jelly Roll Morton, James P. Johnson, Fats Waller, Teddy Wilson, and Art Tatum. This pack covers classic ragtime, early blues and boogie woogie, New Orleans jazz, and more, and includes 14 full songs.

00310882 Book/CD Pack..$16.95

Prices, contents, and availability subject to change without notice.

FOR MORE INFORMATION, SEE YOUR LOCAL MUSIC DEALER,
OR WRITE TO:

HAL•LEONARD®
CORPORATION
7777 W. BLUEMOUND RD. P.O. BOX 13819 MILWAUKEE, WI 53213

Visit Hal Leonard online at
www.halleonard.com

JAZZ PLAY ALONG SERIES

BOOK/CD PACKAGES ONLY $14.95 EACH!

The JAZZ PLAY ALONG SERIES is the ultimate learning tool for all jazz musicians. With musician-friendly lead sheets, melody cues and other split track choices on the included CD, this first-of-its-kind package makes learning to play jazz easier than ever before.

FOR STUDY,
each tune includes a split track with:
- Melody cue with proper style and inflection
- Professional rhythm tracks
- Choruses for soloing
- Removable bass part
- Removable piano part

FOR PERFORMANCE,
each tune also has:
- An additional full stereo accompaniment track (no melody)
- Additional choruses for soloing

DUKE ELLINGTON • Volume 1
Caravan • Don't Get Around Much Anymore • In a Mellow Tone • In a Sentimental Mood • It Don't Mean a Thing (If It Ain't Got That Swing) • Perdido • Prelude to a Kiss • Satin Doll • Sophisticated Lady • Take the "A" Train.
00841644

MILES DAVIS • Volume 2
All Blues • Blue in Green • Four • Half Nelson • Milestones • Nardis • Seven Steps to Heaven • So What • Solar • Tune Up.
00841645

THE BLUES • Volume 3
Billie's Bounce (Bill's Bounce) • Birk's Works • Blues for Alice • Blues in the Closet • C-Jam Blues • Freddie Freeloader • Mr. P.C. • Now's the Time • Tenor Madness • Things Ain't What They Used to Be.
00841646

JAZZ BALLADS • Volume 4
Body and Soul • But Beautiful • Here's That Rainy Day • Misty • My Foolish Heart • My Funny Valentine • My One and Only Love • My Romance • The Nearness of You • (includes lyric sheets).
00841691

THE BEST OF BEBOP • Volume 5
Anthropology • Donna Lee • Doxy • Epistrophy • Lady Bird • Oleo • Ornithology • Scrapple from the Apple • Woodyn' You • Yardbird Suite.
00841689

JAZZ CLASSICS WITH EASY CHANGES • Volume 6
Comin' Home Baby • Blue Train • Footprints • Impressions • Killler Joe • Moanin' • Sidewinder • St. Thomas • Stolen Moments • Well You Needn't (It's Over Now).
00841690

ESSENTIAL JAZZ STANDARDS Volume 7
Autumn Leaves • Cotton Tail • Easy Living • I Remember You • If I Should Lose You • Lullaby of Birdland • Out of Nowhere • Stella by Starlight • There Will Never Be Another You • When Sunny Gets Blue.
00843000

ANTONIO CARLOS JOBIM AND THE ART OF THE BOSSA NOVA Volume 8
The Girl From Ipanema (Garota De Ipanema) • How Insensitive (Insensatez) • Meditation (Meditacao) • Once I Loved (Amor Em Paz) (Love in Peace) • One Note Samba (Samba De Uma Nota So) • Quiet Nights of Quiet Stars (Corcovado) • Slightly out of Tune (Desafinado) • So Danco Samba (Jazz 'N' Samba) • Triste • Wave.
00843001

DIZZY GILLESPIE • Volume 9
Birk's Works • Con Alma • Groovin' High • Manteca • A Night in Tunisia • Salt Peanuts • Shawnuff • Things to Come • Tour De Force • Woodyn' You.
00843002

DISNEY CLASSICS • Volume 10
Alice in Wonderland • Beauty and the Beast • Cruella De Vil • Heigh-Ho • Some Day My Prince Will Come • When You Wish Upon a Star • Whistle While You Work • Who's Afraid of the Big Bad Wolf • You've Got a Friend in Me • Zip-a-Dee-Doo-Dah.
00843003

RODGERS AND HART • Volume 11
The Blue Room • Dancing on the Ceiling • Bewitched • Have You Met Miss Jones? • I Could Write a Book • The Lady Is a Tramp • Little Girl Blue • My Romance • There's a Small Hotel • You Are Too Beautiful.
00843004

ESSENTIAL JAZZ CLASSICS Volume 12
Airegin • Blue Bossa • Ceora • The Frim Fram Sauce • Israel • Joy Spring • Nefertiti • Red Clay • Song for My Father • Take Five.
00843005

JOHN COLTRANE • Volume 13
Blue Train (Blue Trane) • Countdown • Cousin Mary • Equinox • Giant Steps • Impressions • Lazy Bird • Mr. P.C. • Moment's Notice • Naima (Neima).
00843006

IRVING BERLIN • Volume 14
Be Careful, It's My Heart • Blue Skies • Change Partners • Cheek to Cheek • How Deep Is the Ocean (How High Is the Sky) • I've Got My Love to Keep Me Warm • Let's Face the Music and Dance • Steppin' Out with My Baby • They Say It's Wonderful • What'll I Do?
00843007

RODGERS & HAMMERSTEIN Volume 15
Bali Ha'i • Do I Love You Because You're Beautiful? • Hello Young Lovers • I Have Dreamed • It Might As Well Be Spring • Love, Look Away • My Favorite Things • The Surrey with the Fringe on Top • The Sweetest Sounds • Younger Than Springtime.
00843008

COLE PORTER • Volume 16
All of You • Easy to Love (You'd Be So Easy to Love) • From This Moment On • I Get a Kick Out of You • I've Got You Under My Skin • In the Still of the Night • It's De-Lovely • Love for Sale • What Is This Thing Called Love? • You'd Be So Nice to Come Home To.
00843009

Prices, contents and availability subject to change without notice.
FOR MORE INFORMATION, SEE YOUR LOCAL MUSIC DEALER, OR WRITE TO:

HAL•LEONARD® CORPORATION
7777 W. BLUEMOUND RD. P.O. BOX 13819 MILWAUKEE, WI 53213

Visit Hal Leonard online at **www.halleonard.com**

1002